Disclaimer

I am not a Lawyer or an accountant. The information provided in this book should not be mistaken as legal advice in any way. I am only sharing what I know and what has worked for individuals that I know personally. Kimothy M. Wynn and the publisher of this book is not responsible for what you do (or don't do) with the information provided. I make no guarantees of results of the information contained in this book. Kimothy M. Wynn nor the publisher are responsible or liable for any damages including direct, indirect, special, consequential, or punitive damages suffered by any person arising out of the information contained herein.

The views expressed through this book are those of the individual author writing in his capacities only. All liability concerning actions taken or not taken based on the contents of this book are, at this moment, expressly disclaimed. This book's content is provided "as is " no representations are made that the content is error-free.

TABLE OF CONTENTS

CHAPTER 1.............. Introduction to Credit

CHAPTER 2.............. Credit Score

CHAPTER 3.............. Building Credit

CHAPTER 4.............. Debt to Income Ratio

CHAPTER 5.............. Disputing Errors on your Credit Report

CHAPTER 6.............. Interest Rates

CHAPTER 7.............. Credit Dispute Sample Letters

ABOUT THE AUTHOR

From the time I was a teenager up until early adulthood, I had no real concept of credit. Where I grew up in Tacoma Washington, everyone that I knew looked at credit as 'Free Money'. They would apply for J.C. Penny's cards, Macy's cards, and credit cards ... if they were lucky enough to get approved for one, they would 'max it out'. Paying the bill would never cross their minds. It was if there were no consequences in doing that. I didn't know how that could, and would affect the quality of their life later on in life. I'd never heard of TransUnion, Experian, or Equifax. And likewise, I didn't know what a credit bureau was. I also didn't see how a credit bureau would be able to score someone they'd never even met.

I've always wanted to own my own home as well as have my own business. So, when I felt the time was right, I began to do my research. I had no idea that credit was a major factor in whether I could get a home loan or a business loan. I then started to do my research on credit and realized that it was impossible to get any kind of loan with no credit. Needless to say, I was very disappointed. However, during my research on credit I learned how to build it and simplify the process.

Now that I've educated myself on Credit, I feel empowered. And i know that I must share my credit knowledge with everyone who wants to know, everyone that needs to know, and everyone who doesn't know that they should know.

Building Credit is a sure way to improve the quality of your life in almost every aspect. If you have the means, you should get started on building your Credit sooner rather than later.

INTRODUCTION

The goal of the author is to empower others through this easy to follow guide to building credit. By building your credit you can reduce some of the inevitable stresses of life. Through my own personal journey, I've discovered that some of my anxiety was caused by my inexperience with personal finances and credit specifically.

So much of our future is impacted by our credit scores. Our credit scores seriously effect so many areas of our lives that it has the potential to determine whether we're successful in achieving some of the things that you would like to accomplish.

If any of your plans include working towards purchasing a vehicle, owning a home or perhaps one day starting your own business, how you manage your credit can seriously impact those plans. Having bad credit or no credit can be demoralizing to say the least.

Throughout this book you will learn what credit is, how to obtain it and some easy tips on how to build it.

By increasing your understanding of credit, you will achieve a sense of empowerment that can lead to a pattern of success and ultimately aid in your achievement of a secure and responsible future. It's just a fact that when things are easier for you, life can be less complicated.

CHAPTER 1
Introduction to Credit

There are many types of credit. Getting a loan from a Bank, a car loan, a home loan, and credit cards are all different kinds of credit. credit has become a major part of our everyday lives. It has the potential to play a role in whether or not we get approved for an apartment, a house, a car, a smart phone, credit card, a loan from a bank or Credit Union.

If you have a bad credit score when you try to move into a new apartment or home, you will most likely either get denied or end up paying double the amount of deposit than someone with good credit will pay. Most properties are starting to require that you have a 600 Credit score and above to qualify to move into the property. If you have a good credit score and you have the required income, you will most likely get approved anywhere that you apply. A good credit score shows that you are financially responsible and that you pay your bills on time.

A bad credit score shows that you are a risk, that you're financially irresponsible and there's a possibility that you won't pay your bills on time.

If you have no credit, it can be just as bad as having bad credit. With no credit, whatever you get approved for you'll most likely end up paying double the price and higher interest rates for the same things that someone with good credit would pay (we'll go more in depth about this in chapter 7). If you have no credit or bad credit, you'll probably need a Cosigner for almost everything that you wanna do, including applying for a credit card, a loan to buy a home, or a car loan for that vehicle you want. If you have a good credit score and your 'debt to income ratio' (explained in chapter 4) isn't that high, then you'll get approved for all of these kinds of loans easily.

As you can see, credit can affect your life in negative ways as well as in positive ways.

CHAPTER 2
Credit Score

A credit score is what the FICO system uses to rate you on your risk level as well as the likelihood of paying your bills on time. The FICO system keeps collected data from your credit file with the 3 Credit bureau's (TransUnion, Equifax and Experian) to determine your score. Your credit file with those 3-credit bureau's shows and tracks your financial history. It will know if you're current and up to date with paying your bills or if you are behind and late on paying your bills. It will show your Debt to Credit ratio and It will show if you have a history of being behind on your bills, which also can affect your score.

You can go online to annualcreditreport.com, request a FREE Credit Report from all 3 Credit bureau's (TransUnion, Equifax and Experian) to see what's being reported on you. You get 1 free credit report a year from 'annual credit report. com'.

Your FICO score ranges between 300 to 850, with 300 being bad, 850 being the very best that you can get. The things listed below are what goes into calculating up your Credit Score:

* Payment History - makes up 35% of your Credit score.

* Length of Credit History - makes up 15% of your Credit score.

* New Credit - makes up 10% of your Credit score.

* The types of Credit Used - makes up 10% of your Credit score.

* Amounts Owed and/or Credit Utilization - makes up 30% of your Credit score.

PAYMENT HISTORY

Your payment history consists of how you've been using your credit in the past. I call it your 'Credit Track History'. If you've never had anything in your name and have always paid everything on time, you should log onto Creditkarma.com to see what your credit score is. Or just to find out if you have a good, mediocre, or bad Credit score.

LENGTH OF CREDIT HISTORY

It's always good to start building and nurturing your Credit as soon as possible. Fifteen percent of your score is made up of the length of sound financial habits, such as paying all of your bills on time. Twenty-four months is the length of time that a lot of the lenders like to see.

NEW CREDIT

New Credit is pretty self-explanatory. It's just a newly established credit line.

TYPES OF CREDIT USED

Some of your scores are made up from having more than 1 or 2 active lines of credit. It helps your score to have a good mixture of credit cards.

AMOUNTS OWED and/or CREDIT UTILIZATION

This can be tricky because you can be up to date on your credit payments, but your credit score can still go down if you use more than 30% of your total credit limit. In other words, if you have one credit card with a limit of $300, you don't want to spend more than $100 dollars on that credit card. What lenders, as well as the FICO system want to see is that you have an amount of credit extended to you, but that you're not totally dependent upon it. If you keep your credit utilization around 30%, and are on time with your payments, then you can't hurt your score in the credit utilization department.

Now that you know where to go online to see what's being reported on you and exactly goes into calculating your score, we are ready to get started.

CHAPTER 3
Building Credit

Building Credit is not all that complicated. It just takes a combination of having a desire to want good Credit, being attentive to your Credit report, and being proactive in the building of your Credit.

LOG ON TO RENTREPORTERS.com

Normally when you pay your rent-on time every month, it doesn't help build your credit. However, you can log on to 'rentreporters.com' and for a fee, they will report your on-time payments to the 3-credit bureaus.

REVOLVING ACCOUNTS

Revolving account's means opening up multiple lines of Credit. Not simultaneously. it works best if you stagger opening up the Credit lines.

For example, You can log onto Creditkarma.com and apply for a 'Secured Credit Card', but you should Google 'Secured Credit Cards' that report to all three Credit bureau's (Experian, Equifax, and TransUnion), so you can find 3 other companies that offer these kinds of 'Secured Credit Cards'.

Secured means, you'll have to apply for the 'Secured Credit Card', then send the credit card company however much money you want your limit to be. It's 'secured' with the deposit you send them. They usually start at $200. Say you send the Secured Card company $300 dollars; they will send you a 'Secured Credit Card' with a limit of $300 dollars. Activate the card when you get it, and the card is ready to be used to start building your credit.

45 days later. Repeat the process ... but this time get a card from one of the other 'Secured Credit Card' companies that popped up during your Google search. Repeat the process again in another 45 days, so on, and so on, until you have 4 different 'Secured Credit Cards' with 4 different companies that report to all 3 Credit bureaus. By this time, you should check your credit score, it should be on the rise.

Just be mindful to stay around the 30% threshold on all 4 of those 'Secured Credit Cards' combined. For instance, if you have 4 Secured cards with $300 limits, your total sum combined would be $1,200. In order to not go below 30% utilization, you don't want to spend more than $400 total on all 4 of those cards combined. Be sure to pay each Secured credit card bill either before the due date or on the day.

AUTHORIZED USER

If you already know someone who has good Credit, has Credit cards and pays their Credit card bills on time, all the time. Then you can have them fill out the application online with their Credit card company to add you as an 'Authorized User' and as they're being financially responsible by paying their credit card bill on time, it's the same as if you're being financially responsible. As they pay their bill on time every month, your Credit score will start to rise. It's called 'Piggy backing'.

*A note of importance * for all of the parents and guardians out there. If you're building your credit or if you already have good credit, it would be a good idea to add your teenagers (16 years old and up) as authorized users on your credit card and allow them to 'piggy back' off of you. That way, when they are 18 years old and ready to go out in the world, they will be able to be independent since they will already have a good credit score as well as a good payment history.

DOWNLOAD THE 'SELF APP'

The 'Self App' can be an amazing tool to building credit. When you download the 'Self App', follow the instructions on the 'App' on how to get started, once started it will help you begin creating a payment history. The 'Self App' requires a onetime initial administrative payment. Once that fee is paid, you will have everything that the 'Self App' has to offer at your disposal. Self-offers credit builder accounts, secured credit cards and the Self Visa credit card.

These are all easy ways that anyone can create credit, credit history, building up your credit score and enhance the quality of your life, regardless of where you are in life.

CHAPTER 4
Debt to Income Ratio

When a Credit check is run on you, your Credit report and Credit score is what's being examined.

When you apply for a regular Loan, Credit Card, Home Loan, or a Car Loan, the Lender and/or Financial Institution will want to know what your Income is. They will often want to see pay stubs and sometimes ask to see previous tax returns so they can compare your income with the debt that you've accumulated. This is what's commonly known as your 'Debt to Income Ratio'.

The purpose of this is to evaluate you for your ability to repay them If you're approved for the loan or credit card along with all the other debt that they see on your Credit report.

Sometimes a Financial institution/Lender will require you to make 2 or 3 times the amount that you're applying for (even if you have a good credit score). The rationale is, they want to make sure that if something comes up unexpectedly that you'd still be able to make your payment them.

That being said, it would be wise to keep an eye on your own 'Debt to Income Ratio'. That way, you never spread your finances to thin and put yourself in a bind of not being able to pay your bills on time.

The way to figure out your 'debt to income ratio' is to add up all of your monthly expenses/payments and divide it by your bring home pay.

CHAPTER 5
Disputing Errors on Your Credit Report

When you go online and request a copy of your Credit report from annualcreditreport.com, if there is anything on there that doesn't look right to you or that you don't remember, don't hesitate to dispute it by sending a letter stating you want to dispute the negative mark/item (describe the negative item, including the date).

The 3 Credit bureaus are governed by the 'Consumer Financial Protection Bureau' (CFPB). A federal law called the 'Fair Credit Reporting Act' (FCRA) along with the 'Fair Debt Collection Practices Act (FDCPA) form and regulate consumer credit rights in the United States. When you send a dispute letter to the 3 Credit bureau's disputing inaccurate and/or an unfair item, they have 30 days to complete their investigation Per the Fair Credit Reporting Act Section 611(a)(1)(A). Make sure to include the name and account number of the item you are disputing.

The thing is, Credit bureaus are huge companies that rarely complete their investigations within the 30-day allotted time. So, make yourself a copy of the letter, send the Credit bureau the original letter disputing the negative mark/item. Send it Certified Mail Return Receipt so you can track the days from when the Credit bureau receives it. If they don't reply to you within the 30 days then you can write to them and request the negative item be removed per violation of (Fair Credit Reporting Act) Section 611(a)(1)(A).

If you do hear back from the credit bureau claiming the negative item was 'verified', then you should send another letter requesting their 'method of verification' per Fair Credit Reporting Act (FCRA) Section 611(a)(6)(7). It is mandatory that the credit bureau's send you their 'method of verification' within 15 days. This is something they almost NEVER do. So, send the verification request letter Certified Mail Return Receipt, so you will know when they received it. If you don't hear back from them in 15 days, then send a letter requesting them to remove the item per violation of (FCRA) Section 611(a)(6)(7).

It's important when sending letters to Credit bureaus to make a copy for your own records. To always send it Certified Mail Return Receipt, and to write those return receipt numbers on your copies. That's how you end up with the results that you want cause once they violate the (FCRA) policies, it's just easier for them to just remove the negative mark/item rather than to be in violation of federal law.

You can log onto Experian.com/dispute to dispute any inaccurate information or click on the dispute line next to the inaccurate item. Or by using the dispute sample letters. (Dispute Sample Letters in Chapter 7).

CHAPTER 6
Interest Rates

If you have good or an excellent credit score, you'll pay significantly lower interest rates than someone with bad credit or no credit at all.

For example, if you're buying a new car for approximately $30,000 and your credit score is around 600 you may have to pay 12% interest over the course of 72 months. This is due to having a 600-credit score and just so happened to be the best interest rate you could get with that score. Your monthly payments will be somewhere around $587 and by the time you've paid the car off you'll have paid a total of $42,264 for this car.

But If you buy this same car for $30,000 with a 789-credit score at a 2.9% interest rate. You'll pay significantly less. Your monthly payments will be $464 a month and the total amount that you'll ultimately pay for this car will be $32,688.

That is a savings of interest of 9,576 that you can utilize for other things and not have to pay to the banks.

That was for a new car. Let's say you're buying a used car with the same credit score of 600. The used car costs $5,000 at 17.74% interest. With used vehicles, the interest rate dramatically increases for some reason. Let's say the length of the loan is for 72 months. Your monthly payment will be $113. By the time you 'be paid the car off you'll have paid a total of $8,158 for this car.

But if you buy this same vehicle for $5,000 with a better credit score of 789, the interest rate will be at 4.29%. You'll pay significantly less. Your monthly payment will be $79, and the total amount you'll ultimately pay for this car will be $5,680.

If you have a 600-credit score and you're buying a home that costs $300,000 at 9.5% interest because that was the best rate you could get with the 600-credit score, your monthly payments will be 2,414 per month for 30 years. The total cost of your mortgage will be $869,040. You'll pay $569,040 in interest to the banks for this home over the course of 30 years.

Now lets say you have a 789 credit score and you're buying this same house that costs $300,000, you get approved for a 3% interest home loan cause of your great credit score. over the course of the 30 years. Your monthly payments will be 1,265 per month. The total cost of the mortgage is $455,400 at the end of the loan. You'll only pay $155,400 in interest to the banks for this home over the period of those same 30 years.

That is a savings of 413,640 in interest not paid to the banks and left in your pockets to use for other things.

As you can see, in all examples, the person with the 600-credit score paid significantly more than the person with the 789-credit score. The person with the 789-credit score was always able to get a lower interest rate, which in turn allowed him/her to pay less per month as well as the overall amount.

The same concept is real when getting a credit card, getting a loan, and everything else. So, I hope you understand why building and nurturing your credit is so important to your life. It's guaranteed to leave more money in your pockets for other thing's.

CHAPTER 7
Credit Dispute Sample Letters

The addresses to the 3-credit bureaus:

TransUnion, LLC
P.O. Box 2000
Chester, PA 19022

Experian
P.O. Box 4000
Allen, TX 75013

Equifax
P.O. Box 740256
Atlanta, GA 30374

Certified Mail Return Receipt #_____

TransUnion, LLC
P.O. Box 2000
Chester, PA 19022

To whom it may concern:

I was recently denied approval for credit due to a report provided by your company. I am now requesting a credit report from your company.

Per the 'Fair Credit Reporting Act' (FCRA), USC section 1681(g), the credit bureau should send me a copy of my credit report (upon request) due to the fact that I was denied credit within the last 60 days.

Per the 'Fair Credit Reporting Act' (FCRA), 15 USC section 1681(j), this request for a copy should be free of charge and mailed to the address below to.

NAME: (first, middle, and last)

Date Of Birth:

Current Address:

SSN:

Sincerely _____

Certified Mail Return Receipt #_____

Experian
P.O. Box 4000
Allen, TX 75013

To whom it may concern:

I was recently denied approval for credit due to a report provided by your company. I am now requesting a credit report from your company.

Per the 'Fair Credit Reporting Act' (FCRA), USC section 1681(g), the credit bureau should send me a copy of my credit report (upon request) due to the fact that I was denied credit within the last 60 days.

Per the 'Fair Credit Reporting Act' (FCRA), 15 USC section 1681(j), this request for a copy should be free of charge and mailed to the address below to.

NAME: (first, middle, and last)

Date Of Birth:

Current Address:

SSN:

Sincerely _____

Certified Mail Return Receipt #_____

Equifax
P.O. Box 740256
Atlanta, GA 30374

To whom it may concern:

I was recently denied approval for credit due to a report provided by your company. I am now requesting a credit report from your company.

Per the 'Fair Credit Reporting Act' (FCRA), USC section 1681(g), the credit bureau should send me a copy of my credit report (upon request) due to the fact that I was denied credit within the last 60 days.

Per the 'Fair Credit Reporting Act' (FCRA), 15 USC section 1681(j), this request for a copy should be free of charge and mailed to the address below to.

NAME: (first, middle, and last)

Date Of Birth:

Current Address:

SSN:

Sincerely _____

Certified Mail Return Receipt# _____

Equifax
P.O. Box 740256
Atlanta, GA 30374

To whom it may concern:

After reviewing my credit report from your company, I noticed that the negative item/mark listed below is inaccurate. Please delete this inaccurate information immediately to show my true credit history.

Per 'Fair Credit Reporting Act' (FCRA), 15 USC section 1681(i), I am formally disputing this negative item/mark and request that the following information be reverified and removed from my credit file.

Company Name: | Account # | Date on Account | Amount Owed
_____

Federal law states that your company has 30 days from the date your company receives this letter to investigate and reverify the mentioned inaccurate information. Failure to do so requires your company to immediately remove the disputed entry. Per the 'Fair Credit Reporting Act' (FCRA), 15 USC section 1681(j).

Send the verification confirmation to me at the address below:
NAME: (first, middle, and last)

Date of Birth:

SSN:

Address:

Sincerely _____

Certified Mail Return Receipt# _____

Experian
P.O. Box 4000
Allen, TX 75013

To whom it may concern:

After reviewing my credit report from your company, I noticed that the negative item/mark listed below is inaccurate. Please delete this inaccurate information immediately to show my true credit history.

Per 'Fair Credit Reporting Act' (FCRA), 15 USC section 1681(i), I am formally disputing this negative item/mark and request that the following information be reverified and removed from my credit file.

Company Name: | Account # | Date on Account | Amount Owed
_____

Federal law states that your company has 30 days from the date your company receives this letter to investigate and reverify the mentioned inaccurate information. Failure to do so requires your company to immediately remove the disputed entry. Per the 'Fair Credit Reporting Act' (FCRA), 15 USC section 1681(j).

Send the verification confirmation to me at the address below:
NAME: (first, middle, and last)

Date of Birth:

SSN:

Address:

Sincerely _____

Certified Mail Return Receipt# _____

TransUnion, LLC
P.O. Box 2000
Chester, PA 19022

To whom it may concern:

After reviewing my credit report from your company, I noticed that the negative item/mark listed below is inaccurate. Please delete this inaccurate information immediately to show my true credit history.

Per 'Fair Credit Reporting Act' (FCRA), 15 USC section 1681(i), I am formally disputing this negative item/mark and request that the following information be reverified and removed from my credit file.

Company Name: | Account # | Date on Account | Amount Owed
_____

Federal law states that your company has 30 days from the date your company receives this letter to investigate and reverify the mentioned inaccurate information. Failure to do so requires your company to immediately remove the disputed entry. Per the 'Fair Credit Reporting Act' (FCRA), 15 USC section 1681(j).

Send the verification confirmation to me at the address below:
NAME: (first, middle, and last)

Date of Birth:

SSN:

Address:

Sincerely _____

Certified Mail Return Receipt#_____

Equifax
P.O. Box 740256
Atlanta, GA 30374

To whom it may concern:

This letter is in response to your letter claiming that you've reverified the information that I've disputed on my credit report as being accurate.

I now am demanding your company provide me with your company's method of verification of the previously disputed negative item/mark. Your method of verification is to be provided to me within (15) days. Additionally, please provide me with the telephone number, name and person that you contacted regarding the inaccurate information that was disputed by me. Any automated response or e-OSCAR verification is unacceptable.

Please be aware that I am maintaining careful records of my communication with your company for purposes of filing a complaint with the 'Consumer Financial Protection Bureau' for violation of Federal law Wenger v. Trans Union Corp., Case No.95-6445 (C.D.Cal. Nov. 14, 1995).

Failure to respond within 30 days from receipt of this letter may result in small claims action against your company.
You can send your response to me at the address below:

NAME: (first, middle, and last)

Date of Birth:

SSN:

Current Address:

Sincerely _____

Certified Mail Return Receipt#_____

Experian
P.O. Box 4000
Allen, TX 75013

To whom it may concern:

This letter is in response to your letter claiming that you've reverified the information that I've disputed on my credit report as being accurate.

I now am demanding your company provide me with your company's method of verification of the previously disputed negative item/mark. Your method of verification is to be provided to me within (15) days. Additionally, please provide me with the telephone number, name and person that you contacted regarding the inaccurate information that was disputed by me. Any automated response or e-OSCAR verification is unacceptable.

Please be aware that I am maintaining careful records of my communication with your company for purposes of filing a complaint with the 'Consumer Financial Protection Bureau' for violation of Federal law Wenger v. Trans Union Corp., Case No.95-6445 (C.D.Cal. Nov. 14, 1995).

Failure to respond within 30 days from receipt of this letter may result in small claims action against your company.
You can send your response to me at the address below:

NAME: (first, middle, and last)

Date of Birth:

SSN:

Current Address:

Sincerely _____

Certified Mail Return Receipt #_____

TransUnion, LLC
P.O. Box 2000
Chester, PA 19022

To whom it may concern:

This letter is in response to your letter claiming that you've reverified the information that I've disputed on my credit report as being accurate.

I now am demanding your company provide me with your company's method of verification of the previously disputed negative item/mark. Your method of verification is to be provided to me within (15) days. Additionally, please provide me with the telephone number, name and person that you contacted regarding the inaccurate information that was disputed by me. Any automated response or e-OSCAR verification is unacceptable.

Please be aware that I am maintaining careful records of my communication with your company for purposes of filing a complaint with the 'Consumer Financial Protection Bureau' for violation of Federal law Wenger v. Trans Union Corp., Case No.95-6445 (C.D.Cal. Nov. 14, 1995).

Failure to respond within 30 days from receipt of this letter may result in small claims action against your company.
You can send your response to me at the address below:

NAME: (first, middle, and last)

Date of Birth:

SSN:

Current Address:

Sincerely _____

Certified Mail Return Receipt #_____

Equifax
P.O. Box 740256
Atlanta, GA 30374

To whom it may concern:

It's been 30 days since your company received and signed for my dispute letter about the inaccurate information being reported on my credit report by your company.

Attached is a copy of my original letter mailed certified mail return receipt.

Per the 'Fair Credit Reporting Act' (FCRA), 15 USC section 1681(i)(5)(A), your company had 30 days from the date you received my letter to reverify and respond to my request to remove the inaccurate information from my credit file. Therefore, the inaccurate information that's being reported on my credit report could not be verified and must be immediately deleted. Please respond immediately so that I know the item/negative mark has been deleted and not to continue pursuing my legal rights Per 15 USC section 1681(n) and 1681(o).

Please send an updated copy of my credit report showing the item removed to me at the address below:

NAME: (first, middle, and last)

Date of Birth:

Current Address:

SSN:

Sincerely _____

Certified Mail Return Receipt #_____

Experian
P.O. Box 4000
Allen, TX 75013

To whom it may concern:

It's been 30 days since your company received and signed for my dispute letter about the inaccurate information being reported on my credit report by your company.

Attached is a copy of my original letter mailed certified mail return receipt.

Per the 'Fair Credit Reporting Act' (FCRA), 15 USC section 1681(i)(5)(A), your company had 30 days from the date you received my letter to reverify and respond to my request to remove the inaccurate information from my credit file. Therefore, the inaccurate information that's being reported on my credit report could not be verified and must be immediately deleted. Please respond immediately so that I know the item/negative mark has been deleted and not to continue pursuing my legal rights Per 15 USC section 1681(n) and 1681(o).

Please send an updated copy of my credit report showing the item removed to me at the address below:

NAME: (first, middle, and last)

Date of Birth:

Current Address:

SSN:

Sincerely _____

Certified Mail Return Receipt #_____

TransUnion, LLC
P.O. Box 2000
Chester, PA 19022

To whom it may concern:

It's been 30 days since your company received and signed for my dispute letter about the inaccurate information being reported on my credit report by your company.

Attached is a copy of my original letter mailed certified mail return receipt.

Per the 'Fair Credit Reporting Act' (FCRA), 15 USC section 1681(i)(5)(A), your company had 30 days from the date you received my letter to reverify and respond to my request to remove the inaccurate information from my credit file. Therefore, the inaccurate information that's being reported on my credit report could not be verified and must be immediately deleted. Please respond immediately so that I know the item/negative mark has been deleted and not to continue pursuing my legal rights Per 15 USC section 1681(n) and 1681(o).

Please send an updated copy of my credit report showing the item removed to me at the address below:

NAME: (first, middle, and last)

Date of Birth:

Current Address:

SSN:

Sincerely _____

IN CONCLUSION

If you've sent the sequence of the dispute letters in this chapter and find that the credit bureaus have not removed the negative item/mark from your credit report, but they are in violation of Federal law by not responding in the allotted time or not sending you the reverification that you requested. The last step is to go online and file a complaint with the 'CONSUMER FINANCIAL PROTECTION BUREAU' (CFPB) at www.consumerfinance.gov/complaint, or by writing them at the address below.

Thoroughly Explain and attach a copy of the sequence of dispute letters that you've sent to all 3 credit bureaus. Express in your complaint that they are in violation of Federal law by not responding or deleting the negative item/mark that you've disputed within the allotted time frame under Federal law. And watch how that negative item/mark seems to mysteriously disappear in about 2 to 4 weeks from your credit report.

Address:

Consumer Financial Protection Bureau
1700 G. Street N.W.
Washington, DC 20552

www.ingramcontent.com/pod-product-compliance
Lightning Source LLC
Chambersburg PA
CBHW070846220526
45466CB00002B/903